The Unspoken Word

Written by Antoinette Van Sluytman

Obavan Dzine
Risk It All Design   Studios and Gallery

Co Editors and Designers for The Unspoken Word

ISBN:1718765029
ISBN-13 9781718765023

DEDICATION

To my parents, for always believing in me and being my fuel, my sister for always inspiring me and offering me honest feedback, my brother for always encouraging me to achieve my goals. Also, to Professor Ambers, for being my mentor and honorary grandfather, and to all the intellectuals and revolutionaries who are not afraid to speak up for change. I write for the people, and I attempt to capture the spirit of the struggle within my writing. I acknowledge all those before me who have used the tip of a pen/pencil to fight against oppression and racism and have empowered the masses with the Unspoken Words of the revolution.

Table of contents

Author Rights

All content expressed within the following poetry and spoken word are the opinions solely belonging to the author who attempts to reflect her social, political, and revolutionary thoughts on the many topics concerning the African American experience. These opinions are meant to speak out against oppression, racism, mental ignorance, as well as invoke self-criticism and empowerment as a means to aid our progression. Again, the author's opinions are her own and any disagreement or agreement, reflects the opinion of solely the individual reading. Feel free to express your own thoughts privately, the opinions expressed by any individual will be respected as the opinions of the author is expected to be. Furthermore, this is conscious revolutionary writing, therefore intellectual interpretation and political dialogue is expected.

Personal statement
Antoinette Van Sluytman

"A people without knowledge of their past history, origin, and culture is like a tree without roots," once said the great Pan-Africanist leader, Marcus Mosiah Garvey, who is one of the many historical Black leaders who have inspired my early life with his words.

Having been brought up in a highly focused home schooled environment by well-educated parents, with an inherited family library of classic African/African American literature at my disposal, African American/African history has always been a big part of my life. My homeschooled education has severed my ties to any kind of distractions a Highschool social life would've offered me, such as peer pressure and the brainwashing effects of institutional racism, therefore transformed me into a highly concentrated and mature individual who has had an early start into developing my creative passions into tangible goals. Most importantly, my home school education has grounded me in the truth of my history and has focused me on the important factors that can further better my life as a young African American woman.

History has become an essential theme that I incorporate into all my different passions. The importance of Africana history is the empowerment it contains. I have faced many years of frustration over the lack of African American children books at bookstores. I was constantly struggling to find African American teen books that didn't contain the same kind of derogatory stereotypes that I was used to seeing in the media. This is what inspired me to write my own African American children book and to maintain my focus in my education in history.

My education in history first started with my home school education which incorporated heavy African American historical literature and lecturing, this then transferred to my involvement with the African Latin Museum "Casa Del Rey Moro," located in Old Town, San Diego. The African Latin museum, owned by Professor Chuck Ambers, is where much of my historical knowledge bloomed. By taking frequent trips to the museum, I advocated much of my time to studying ancient African civilizations at the museum, which mainly developed from my interest in researching Kemet history.

The times when I wasn't drawing or doing my home school, I'd always be found reading historical books. Eventually, I began to explore writing.

From the many years of developing my skills as a writer and artist I have received numerous awards for my work. For an example, I am a "Gold key" winner of the 2017 "Scholastic art and writing competition" in the section of art, and a "Silver key" winner in the section of poetry. My art has been chosen to be published numerous times in the "Celebrating art" competition anthology, and one of my poems is a semi-finalist in the "Poetry Nation Competition," and was selected to be published in their anthology, "Upon arrival." Besides receiving many awards at a young age, I have also participated in many cultural events.

With my involvement with the "Casa Del Rey Moro" museum, opportunities for me to share my knowledge began to present themselves. At the age of twelve, I presented a historical presentation in conjunction with the museum about the steps of Kemet mummification, at the Jacob Center in San Diego. I had the opportunity to do another presentation for "Casa Del Rey Moro" at the Balboa Park, "Mingei International Museum" about the future of Black dolls. I also did another presentation about the involvement of African American women in STEM, at the "Northrop Grumman aerospace museum," and another at a Chule Vista High school about the female pharaoh, Queen Hatshepsut, in honor of Black history month.

My art has also been chosen to be shown at the "History and Hairshow, 400 years without a comb" exhibit in Escondido San Diego, at the 2016 Grossmont College Hyde student art exhibit, and I was selected to have my art auctioned at the "Legacy in Black" event at the Balboa Park "History Center," hosted by the "San Diego African American Museum of Fine Art" (SDAAMFA) and "Black Xpression."

My educational goals for the future involve my love for writing and drawing which both incorporate Black History. Through my art I will give others like me a positive image of themselves.

The lack of knowledge of our history is because much of African American/African history is ignored by the public-school system due to institutional racism. With my education, I will teach true African American/African history through my literature, my art, and my voice. Also with my studies in creative writing, business, and art, I will build more opportunities for other people like me by creating my own business. At a young age I was taught how important education is to the world, and with my education I am prepared to make changes and create better opportunities for not just myself, but for others.

Antoinette Van Sluytman
5/4/2018
California

I am the root, my words are the tree, my poetry is the fruit, my people are the birds.

– Antoinette Van Sluytman

Proud Banners of Death

"Proud banners of death" Langston Hughes once wrote in his

"Tomorrow's Seed".

The red on your flag is the blood that my people bleed.

And the striped bars across its tapestry,

Are the metal bars used to imprison me.

Is the blue the color of democracy?

That included all free men but they Jim Crowed me?

Are the stars the glowing lights of lady liberty.

Who never raised her torch for me.

The needle sewn into the flag's colors,

Stabbed the wounds of slavery.

Proud banners of death raised before a slave shack.

Red, white, and blue but there was never the color black.

Dark bodies lay beneath the soil and sea.

So forgive me if I don't salute Robert.E. Lee.

The white slave master who caught our John Brown.

Who died fighting for freedom but no statue of him to be found.

White terrorists have been elected to office since Columbus

times,

But we think marching will make them apologize for their

crimes.

We sing the same song in different eras,

To the same face,

But they will never stop oppressing us,

Because they know that we are a powerful race.

For the white power structure, we will only ever be equal,

If we just stay in our place.

The American Dream,

Is a world where no black people are to be seen.

They will chant "home of the brave!"

When they wave proud banners of death above my grave.

Tomorrow's seed,

Will begin to bleed,

The true colors of the American Flag.

And we will find the burnt remnants,

Of a bloody rag.

Home of the coward

And the unfree.

Land of the poor

And hypocrisy.

That bled it's lies into me.

But the star spangled banner was the last thing my ancestors

saw,

Before you hung her on that tree.

And when we burn your flag,

And wake up from the terrors of your American dream.

Dark bodies will rise.

And show you what the land of the Brave, And the Free,

Actually means to me.

We Rise

Are you awake?

No seriously, brothers and sisters,

Do you see the bright lights put up to blind your mind,

Shining stars and illusions high above our eyes.

Silicone chains on our wings so we can't fly,

Are you awake? Cuz there's white poison concentrated into dye.

There a war for you mind.

Deception has been created to keep us blind.

Wrapping us up in stereotypes and categories in glossy binders.

Covering our eyes with glossy pages from magazines like blinders.

Look past your bodies liberation.

For if your mind lacks emancipation,

You are a link in the chain of our mental incarceration.

There ain't no debate.

But brothers and sisters are you awake?

Look carefully into the stone eyes of your ancestors,

Can you see the pride recorded on their breasts?

Can you see the blood on the hands of the priest who painted their faces

white,

Picked up a chisel and said,

"I'll make their noses right"

Disregarded our people's right,

Taught our people the faces of our black kings and queens in false light?

My soul glows bright,

As their lies increase height,

For my destiny is to begin this fight,

My people were made to create,

To lead, To cultivate,

The mind ,body and spirit.

This fight is for us to inherit.

I will be free from mental incarceration and dependency,

For I do not fear death.

I fear the life of a simplistic victim who has not contributed to her

people.

I will honor my ancestors, who raised their people into citizens of great

empires.

Cuz, I'm sick of seeing little black girls in the reflections of dirty glass,

One black girl out of twenty sitting beside me in class,

Overplayed coons in mass,

Deep down I know we gotta change this fast.

And if I die without completing this task,

Tell Queen Hatshepsut I tried to honor her mask,

Tell Assata Shakur I tried to regain our past,

Tell Kathleen Cleaver,

I stood tall like she did,

Maybe, I dunno, but I think I'm more than just a kid,

I think I'm a chosen disciple of what they did,

And I am ready,

For the movement of the Black Nation,

To begin.

One last question,

Are you read for black progression?

But before we can begin that debate.

Ask yourselves,

Are you awake?

Cuz it's time to get woke.

Precious Yellow Fruits

Smile, gawk, and adore- you love everything that does not represent the

Moor.

Adulation, degradation, separation, the burden of a nation.

You made my skin the badge to win.

Cuz it ain't dark like a sin.

I do not wear my light skin with pompous pride.

It doesn't give me satisfaction for you to see pass my Black side.

A white badge of privilege to make my sisters turn their backs to me.

Because of white beauty standards this is how it has to be.

But no.

I will not give you the appreciation,

To see me so inclined towards separation,

From the powerful Blackness that makes me sing.

Instead of the luck that my skin is the same color as your buttercream.

Because my skin isn't sweet and dark like a grape.

But the color of my skin is the result of my great Grandmother's rape.

So don't smile, gawk, and beam.

Because my skin isn't the same color as your coffee bean.

Painted by the ignorant colors of history.

Mulatto, Creole, an exotic mystery.

So don't call me beautiful and her a "Hot Tottie."

Cuz I have the "privilege" to know a white man invaded my

Grandmother's body.

What do they see as I strut in my fro?

They whisper and stare saying.

"Wow, would you look at that light skinned nigger go!"

"She sure put on a show."

For the little black girls, I do it to inspire.

But for some reason they seeing something higher.

An envious expression to my creamy complexion.

Toni came out right cuz her skin was light.

An endless fight,

Against the standards of white.

As my burning anger increases height.

But deep down, I acknowledge the privileges I have that others lack.

The privileges my cousins will never have, cuz their skin is too black.

Smile, Gawk, and adore!

Why can't you acknowledge what you ignore!?

Wrenched in their guts deep,

I can see the hate begin to seep.

Black face, Dark race, Self hate.

Bet your cards they'll never make it far!

But I say, don't kneel, don't beg, don't pray,

For god to make your skin lighter some day.

Don't disfigure, don't cover, to change your hue.

But all I hear is-- "Oh gawd! If only my greatest grandmother got

violated too!"

Smile, gawk, and adore- but be careful what you wish for.

Marvel at my light skinned fame.

But what I saw in the reflection was the descendant of another woman

pain.

I once hated my straight nose, my fair skin, and my freckled face.

For I had no pride in resembling even an inch of the white man's race.

But now, you can gawk, smile, call me a diva.

For I am nothing but a strong and independent BLACKTINA.

Ancient Clay

Old town's human zoo, shows a woman of ancient clay.

Her skin is a brown hue, and a wrinkled display.

They shape her destiny like that aged clay,

and sell it behind a glass window,

paying 50 cents a day.

Beneath her wrinkled brow a sourness can be found.

A soul woven into the tapestry of Mexican blankets,

sold on a corner street where only silence is the sound.

The Old Town human zoo,

displays a woman without a dime,

who serves the drunk white boys her garbs and wine.

If you look carefully to your right,

you will behold a sight,

at the back of every restaurant's cave,

you will find an Aztec slave.

"Pat" "Pat" "Pat"

She makes your tortillas and bakes your bread.

Maybe a crumb or two could keep her children fed.

You wear her culture then toss it into a pit.

You turned her identity into a label on your sweet hot chocolate.

You paint the skulls of her dead ancestors.

The ancestors of your romanticized Maria.

Wonder do you, what is that salty taste in my tortilla?

No matter if her children may suffer every year,

I didn't pay to consume an Aztec woman's tears.

Ha! Ha! Ha!

Watch her clean my floor!

Look at her raggedy children,

Nameless and poor.

Behold the Old Town zoo.

For 5 cents a day you can witness a descendant of human pain.

Wonder do you,

Is that soap and water she scrubs on your floor?

Or the tears she wept for the Native Americans massacred upon

America's shores.

Did you enjoy this tour?

I've hear this story a million times before.

It disgusts me to the core.

That once a day, a clay woman is put on display.

She is not a tango dancer.

Or a stereotypical figurine.

Some forget she is even a human being.

400

They will tell the tail,

Of a nation,

So brave, so tall,

They will say,

They were Black,

The creators of all,

A people,

Who defied extinctions call,

Who survived the gutters of corruption,

Racism,

Oppression,

Incarceration,

Slavery,

The slums of human heartaches,

Eras of genocide,

They strived for justice,

They were the Black race,

They will say,

That they could paint a city gold,

With empty hands,

That they could paint a city gold,

In lands of plundered waste.

They will tell a tail,

Of a people,

Who came up from nothing,

They were Black,

They will say,

And none,

Could ever keep them down.

Ancestry

The colored palette beneath your skin,

Shows me the shaded patterns and convoluted fibers, of my existence.

Pure untouchable connection you pulled from the star-lit sky,

And drew our anatomy from the constellations.

Our arms were like gnarled roots bearing fruits to the next generation.

Our feet were like wings, carrying us across unconceivable distances.

Our souls were like the sun, an untouchable virtue of life.

Can you romanticize the truth so much that it is no longer believable?

Look closer.

Truth bears in the time chiseled into rock,

Of walking gods who bled red blood,

And painted it across the scarlet blue sky.

Can I walk with them one last time?

To feel,

To see,

To conceive,

What it truly means,

To be a human being.

Satin Casket

When I opened my eyes,

I saw my picture on the front page of the news.

My name in bold font- my eyes a liquid reflection,

Of that ordinary picture, of an ordinary Negro girl.

When I opened my eyes,

They were writing books about me, in standard font.

To be opened and closed at their leisure,

Of women weeping over a satin casket.

Their tears worth twenty dollars.

When I opened my eyes,

I smelled flowers,

I heard them shouting my name,

I saw them painting my face on brick walls.

When I opened my eyes,

I remembered the opal eyes of a pale snake,

Coiling around me.

I wondered why my mother wept.

When I opened my eyes,

I saw Emmett Till,

Singing songs of Sweet Chariots,

And mother's embrace.

When I opened my eyes,

I wondered.

How did I become so loved?

So famous in America?

Then I looked closer,

And observe the color red.

And realized finally,

That it is because I am dead.

Niña Del Sol

Piers of gold, retrieved from the caves of life and divine creation,

Brought before the world in your glorious ebony skin like the night sky,

Against your white teeth like a necklace of bright stars,

Thick lips so beautiful,

And complete like the powerful iridescence of a full moon,

The lovely full lips sculpted into the wise faces of your magnificent ancestors.

May you kiss away the pain in your mama's eyes.

Nappy hair, so thick and breathtaking like a sculpted crown from your dark scalp.

Black curls kiss your neck like the mighty lion's mane,

And the stunning green trees that bare us your fruit of life.

May your crown grow larger like coils of pride reaching towards the sun.

Nappy, nappy, nappy, oh how I love your nappy hair.

Broad nose, wide like the horizon that the sun caresses,

Big just like your heart of steel and hips of pride.

Big like your soul that glows brighter than the sun.

Little girl of fire, your pride and love is the redemption in our stone hearts,

You are a walking reflection of our mothers of glory and queens of triumph.

Some do not see the beauty that you behold little girl with the big hair,

And you are taught not to see it either.

But little black butterfly,

I see your true glorious perfection.

You are a young warrior queen.

Black like your mother,

And your mother's mother.

Little bird of the sun, oh how I love your black skin,

Your nappy hair,

Your thick thighs,

Your broad nose,

And your soul of fire.

None, is the barrier that you cannot break.

Dear black bird,

You are not ugly,

Society is.

Blacker Berry Woman.

The birth of the Black nation lies between the legs of a blacker berry woman.

The rise of the Black nation lies between the knowledge and experience of her words.

The Blacker Berry woman raised the Black men into fighter, into scholars, into poets, into artists, into kings, into fathers.

If the Black nation falls, it is because the Black Woman has been severed from here pride.

And so they have bred a new type of Black Woman.

One that is yellow,

One that is brown,

One that is red,

One that is Passo Blanco.

And one that hates herself so much that it would only make sense for her to teach her children how to hate themselves to.

But if you look closely,

You can see the blacker berry woman still in them.

Not in the boldness of their noses,

Nor in the wideness of their hips,

Nor in the loud way they speak,

Nor in the thickness of their lips.

But in the undeniable strength and unbreakable pride,

Within their blacker berry souls.

The power to lift a nation back onto its feet.

Lies in the strength of her embrace, and the conscious divinity of her

soul.

Rise Black woman.

So your blacker berry daughters,

Can raise soldiers too,

And begin the reconstruction,

Of the Black Woman's nation.

The Exposed Woman

Why should I hide?

Do the breasts that offer you the milk that builds your back and fills you

with sustenance shame you?

The same breasts from which you suckled,

where the exposed Woman offered you life.

Does it make you uncomfortable?

Does it make you embarrassed to know that the growth from adolescence

to "The Man"

you revere with pride in your chest,

relies on the suckled nutrients provided by the breasts of an exposed

Woman?

Then why should I hide?

Does it bother you to see her exposed back?

The back she carried you on for four hundred years through the filth and

the merciless hands dripping with greed;

through the cotton plantations and fields.

The back that was burdened with the lash of oppression and the labels of

her gender,

the scars upon the raw, tender, and rigid lines and curves of her back revealed upon the auction block.

The back that was beat but never bent as she carried you on.

And why should I hide?

Does the flower between her legs make you cover your eyes?

The womb that cracked and expanded enough times to birth generations

and nations, the womb violated by the same man you worship, the womb

of an exposed Woman?

So why should I hide?

Gaze upon the anatomy of a god which birthed the strongest Men and

Women, the nations of the world, the life we see.

You may blush, you may gasp, or you may glance away in discomfort.

But I will not hide, because you too were born from an exposed Woman.

Fallen Angel

Mind over body.

The chains may be unbreakable, but was the savage's heart too wild to be tamed?

Too civilized to become an animal.

When the savage knows who he is, the body is the only thing that is chainable.

All signs are there. Branded flesh, dark skin, nappy hair.

But what you cannot see, is the free entity, of a slave.

Is that the savage already knows who he is.

Everything has been prepared.

The shackle, the whip, the chains, the cabin.

But what you cannot see, is his free pride.

While the master sits on his throne.

The savage remembers his own.

"What have we done wrong?" They ask.

It is, that the savage already knows who he is.

"Why liberty or death?" They ask.

It is, because the savage remembers the soil of Africa.

And the voices of his kin.

So when the whip lashes,

He pulls his soul within.

Untouched.

They had all the makings for the perfect slave.

 But what they didn't realize,

Was that the savage already knows who he is.

A lost brother,

son and father.

A lost king in the diaspora of hate and hypocrisy.

A Black angel who fell from Africa.

A God in the fire pits of human exploitation.

And so his soul returned to Africa.

Because she knew who he was too.

Black Panthers

When God,

Sent his Angels,

To avenge their King.

On an eerie night,

Diseased pigs wearing badges,

Squealed and screamed.

For his Angels,

Cloaked in black,

Shot arrows of light into the sky,

Their fists belonged to heaven,

To avenge their King's dream.

Their hair was soft like clouds,

And blacker than the dark ocean in the sky,

They wore nothing but black,

And the filthy pigs hide.

They preached freedom,

And wore the garbs of justice,

So beautiful was their sacred verbs,

Spoken from god,

Who cleansed the ghettos,

Of fascist pigs carrying lightning rods.

May they never forget,

The tail of the Angels of God,

Who slayed the pigs,

Screaming POWER TO THE PEOPLE,

May the courage in their hearts never die.

And I saw God smiling,

When they returned to the sky.

The Last Generation

I'm a soldier raised for a battle that has been fought for 400 years.

Little do they know the strength of their fear.

I am their living nightmare in a world I can only hear.

Little do they know that we are the last generation,

Bigger than the largest migration,

And too dumb for the prize of their education.

They shoot down our communities and wave white flags,

But the surrender is an illusion,

And equality is a hallucination.

This is the last generation.

It never started with a dream, but a reality.

We are what's left of the Black mentality.

Free children speak words of insanity.

We are the last generation.

Beneath their respectability.

But even a quarter of the Black mentality,

Can conquer and repel oppressive white supremacy,

Open your eyes,

To the spectrum of the colored people's mind.

Then rise.

The last generation will cross that final line.

And make America great for the very first time.

Freedom's Asylum

I seek insanity in a world where we are taught to accept a simplistic mentality as sanity.

I am bred to be lonely,

For freedom is insanity,

An impenetrable mind and soul. You cannot understand the insane.

They are too connected to their souls;

They seek beyond minimum wages and plaques,

above their buried bodies.

Bravery and insanity aren't much different,

Away from the soulless humans below for so long,

The thought of sanity is that of a subordinate, simplistic, individual,

Below the standards of the human being.

We are born insane...

The mind cannot accept the mindless chatter.

And the mindless chatter cannot accept the mind.

Only insanity can save humanity.

Trials of Justice

If justice truly existed.

She is the abused subject, In the household of America.

If justice truly existed.

She is a heinous creature,

Who forfeit her promises, to a nation.

 If justice truly existed.

She is the sores on our back that reminds us that justice,

Never served those who are Black.

Colin Kaepernick

Was not the width of your shoulders,

Nor the strength of your arms,

That cried justice's name,

On the grassy fields of complacent guts and glory.

Was it the courage of your heart,

The strength of your soul,

That cried justice's name,

in silent arenas?

Was it the tint of your skin,

The length of your nose,

The mass of your hair,

That made you ineligible to cry justices name?

Will it be the Black Pride in your step,

The untouchable love for your people,

The eye for justice,

That they will crucify you for?

Was your complexion accepted,

when you silently kept to your plays?

But color will always be a problem,

when you cry justice's name.

When you exposed their racism,

Did you risk your fame?

When you removed your helmet,

And walked away,

One look could tell you,

That you never had the right,

To call justice's name.

Forbidden Love

I am in awe at his energy,

His power,

The beauty of the jagged black and white lines,

that stripe across his features,

I am in love with his strength,

The broadness of his figure,

The bold pride,

In his blackness,

The dark scars,

Lining the curved shapes,

of his broad back,

He carries the weight of a thousand people.

I am enthralled by the resilience in his eyes,

The promise of his grace,

The scent of his presence,

Like sweet cologne in the air. We will marry in the hills of freedom,

Where I will paint his colors,

Across black canvases. He is my first love.

He is the resistance,

The black revolution,

And I am in love with him.

White Ink

To the bravest soul.

That seeks explanation.

Is it the pen or sword?

That drives a nation.

Pen writes laws,

Laws write history,

History counts numbers,

Of dead black and brown bodies.

That what they called a mystery.

What the pen writes.

The sword follows.

What the pen says.

The masses swallow.

The pen kills.

The pen inspires.

The pen manipulates.

The pen glorifies liars.

What her pen has written.

The sword is perhaps,

The slave,

To the hands behind ink.

She writes the standard,

Of how we are to think.

Behind the screens,

Of humanity's most heinous deeds,

To the bravest soul,

Will find behind mahogany desks,

On the eve of freedom's resistance,

A classic white man,

Who wrote evil into existence.

Silent Walls

Seeking answers beyond my soul,

got me finding lies on the other line of the phone.

Drifting souls singing whack lines for white dimes.

Any woman can sell her life for stones and paper.

But my spirit grows faster than my skin.

Times running out,

And will I get a chance to proceed?

Voice and knowledge gets me right,

Skinny arms and cute face won't get me far.

I see the battle behind black screens,

And white paper.

All I can do is watch number increase,

And mothers' scream.

Voice and hair only does so much for those with stone hearts.

Times running out and all I do is watch.

But can you hear me?

Seeds of Hate

The renaissance of the mind and body,

Is still yet to be emancipated from ingrained toleration,

Of white oppression and materialistic illusions.

I speak with the eye behind the camera,

That has seen the hate and respite,

for the black skin of children of mental slavery and oppression.

They wish for an egalitarian system,

with neglect for their ancestor's attempts to-

eradicate,

contain,

and dominate the original principles of the human seed.

Though our minds have been contorted and misguided,

The original mind is a puissant purpose,

brewed deep with the beauty and grandiose roots of the Black mind,

A mind forced to be contorted and compressed,

into materialistic fascination, and badges of death and murder,

but instead reanimated into a new brand, of purpose.

I ask, if they must complain so adamantly how detached they are from

their white ancestors,

in their path of glorifying the blood, of hung Black children,

then why do they not stand with us in the fight,

against modern white imperialism, and supremacy?

They are the hands behind the whip that lashed at my greatest mother's

back;

They shoot a Black body for stealing a purse,

while they rob the world of its glory and culture,

White children of imperialistic evil do not contain the courage to prove

their disconnection,

from the benefits of Black and Native American bloodshed,

 For they reap the benefits of wealth and white privilege.

But the children of slavery,

see their hypocrisy,

and their reenactment of mental slavery,

for we have already begun to build our own mountain,

to regain our glory,

and purpose.

Our separation and retaliation is inevitable.

Because of their neglection,

Of our oppression,

And their silence,

To the violence.

We waste no time on their pointless inquiry.

For unity,

Is an impossible theory.

Cowards With Dice

A coward is a dope dealing rapper,

Who would rather remain in the comfort and simplicity of singing

harmful words and messages to Black people,

rather than speak out against topics that are affecting them.

Who would rather call a black man a "Nigger" than call a white man a

racist.

Who would rather call a black woman a "bad bitch" than call America

sexist.

Who would rather spend money on strip clubs then invest in the Black

communities and build Black businesses.

Who would rather sing about sex, money, and drugs to children rather

than education, self-esteem, and Black pride.

Who would rather benefit financially off of calling his own people

derogatory words than speak out against White supremacists and racism.

A coward is a dope dealing rapper.

Who is a slave to money.

Who sings about giving women all his money and keys then complains

about gold diggers.

Who grins like a coon but thinks it's cool because he wears a grill.

Who encourages young boys to grow up thinking that calling women vulgar words is okay.

Who is ignorant of his history and roots.

Who is used to smother the voices of the righteous.

A coward is a dope dealing rapper.

Who is a slave to the system.

Changing Winds

Hurricanes kissed these lands,

Unwrapping the width of mother's wrath,

She marks the death of her inhabitants at 10:40;

The storms in the constellations awaken from nightmares of silent triggers,

with babies stuck in the barrels of mother's shotgun.

Father told me not to go outside for fear of floating cocaine needles.

I could be swept by mother's long arms, Into the merciless pounding of her heart.

I could drown in the gun powder, pouring from the sky.

Or perhaps father fears the smog that mothers breathes from her lungs.

She cleansed her land with a fearsome strike.

Her children begged to leave just one factory.

I wanted to observe her wrath one last time.

To observe her hurricane kisses.

In the process I could get swept by her long arms,

But I just wanted to see mother's glory, and wave goodbye.

Before she returned to the sky.

Eye Of The Storm

I can see the storm.

She calls to me,

She brews within,

She is powerful,

She sleeps within my blood cells,

And pumps inside my heart,

Look closer,

And you can see her,

Staring at you,

From the matter of paper and pencil.

Constellations in my Skin

Women of my brown skin,

My black hair,

My veins,

And my mahogany eyes.

Goddess of my fingernails,

My sweat,

My wounds,

And my fears.

I see the patterns of constellations,

Painted into the tapestry of your skin,

And witness the true beauty,

Of God.

1 And 1

Underneath my skin,

Is a soul you cannot understand.

Save the apologies,

I'm a limit breaker.

Can't remember how it began,

But I know how it'll end.

Because I am the second chance.

Amerikkkan Anthem

Hear we toil the lands of the dark-skinned race,

The lands here we call Amerikkka.

Here lay the bodies of our chiefs,

Who fought the devils,

Sent by the old king.

In the lands here we call Amerikkka.

Where they hung us on trees,

Until we couldn't breathe,

And did horrible things,

That you couldn't even conceive.

In the lands we call Amerikkka.

Here in the lands where they lie, lie, lie.

And mock freedoms name.

Is the land here we call Amerikkka.

Where the land of the free,

Belongs to liars,

And thieves.

American Veteran

Under the gun,

I count twenty one foot soldiers,

Running up a hill of fallen limbs,

Smoking cigars under ancient lynching trees.

Driving fast cars into slave graveyards.

In the barrel of the gun,

I count two hundred rolling heads,

A blood splattered flag waving over the dead bodies of black children.

Drinking liquor inside a prison cell,

Singing songs about money and overseer sirens.

My finger on the trigger.

Reminds me of the fire burning in my chest,

Where blood and broken bone bubbles,

Under oppression,

Smearing pain, pleasure, and plastic on my face,

So when they see me at least they see the powder over my skin,

And not the shame in my eyes.

Living life so fast the tears never dry.

In fact my life is like gasoline,

And the gun is my spark,

Where my life will finally ignite,

Into the person this country hates so much.

The person everyone is taught to fear.

But at least they'll finally see me.

Someone will finally say I was here.

Under the gun of America.

In the gutters of her chamber.

With my name as her engravement.

Even though to them,

I'll just be another black body,

laying on the pavement.

Beloved Mine

Stuck inside a cranium,

Round and round,

Vision triple it,

Geniuses can trip too,

Don't forget what she do,

Is twice as much as you,

Stuck in this cycle,

Of hate vs love,

Beloved my fingers,

Beloved my hands,

Beloved my cranium,

Though if only,

They could just fly away,

And carry me with them.

Because I am only here.

Stuck inside my cranium.

And inside of it,

Is a lot of things you'll never understand,

Stuck inside a dream,

Wring my arms outside,

Until I fly,

And I don't care if I die.

Cuz I stuck inside a cranium.

Writing you a poem,

That you'll never understand,

Beloved my breath,

Beloved my eyes,

Beloved my dreams,

And still I cry.

Cuz I stuck inside a cranium.

Fly or die.

Goddess in my Mirror

We are born with the burden the thieves of our herstory have granted us.

We are the only ones who can acknowledge our own pain.

We are the only ones who can refuse to stay the same.

We are the only ones who can hear our sister's silenced screams.

We are the only ones who can sob for our grandmother's broken dreams.

We are the only ones who can hold on to our humanity.

We are the only ones who can claim our sanity.

Only when this is accomplished, will the Black and Brown Woman

become the greatest and most powerful living soul on earth.

Only then will our daughters put the shards together, and in the heart of

the mirror, in all of our reflections we will see the most beautiful and

extravagant Black Goddess and Queen the world has ever seen.

Only then will our grandmothers finally rest.

I can see the storm of the Black Goddess coming.

Tarbaby

Tears of the Black musician,

Fills the cups of the Tarbabies.

Tap dancers, dancing across the minefields of racism,

Show the Tarbabies where to walk.

Jazz singers, singing from the branches of lynching trees,

Show the Tarbabies how to feel.

Sunday preachers, grasping the cold hands of crucified angels,

Teach the Tarbabies how to hold on.

Young black panthers, prowling in the jungles of hatred,

Teach the Tarbabies how to fight.

The pen of the Negro writer, writing across blood splattered pages.

Teach the Tarbabies the experience of the black struggle.

And from the musician's cup of tears,

The Tarbabies built wells of holy water.

And from walking across the minefields of racism successfully,

The Tarbabies grew fields of spring flowers,

And from learning how to feel,

The Tarbabies preached soul,

And from learning how to hold on,

The Tarbabies reached out to others,

And from learning how to fight,

The Tarbabies built forts of pride,

And from learning the experiences of the black struggle,

The Tarbabies,

Became free.

Banished Dream

Breathtaking,

Of the things unsaid,

Of the words unseen,

Perhaps unspoken topic,

Boil in my open skull,

Where my demons scream.

You can't understand,

The things they say inside of me,

Swallowing bitter fruit,

Breathtaking,

To hold back words is a sin;

So beware when I release them,

Bag em out,

Keem em in,

Spit it out,

Eat rotten fruit,

Swallow the seeds,

And pray to god they grow.

But what you cannot see,

Is that I'm the ghost,

Of a generation's

banished dream.

American Crisis

Why allow racism to breed?

To corrupt the world with it's hateful seeds.

Poisoning the white communities with hatred and bigotry,

Now how deep rooted can it be?

So invisible how can they see?

Brought into the cult of racism

still runs deep in their history.

So they won't let us go

even when we say "We can't breath"

A disease running through their cells

And in their bloodstream.

So powerful I don't have to be guilty

for them to shoot me.

Even with my hands up

my color is all they'll ever see in me.

Because racism was aloud to breed.

It lives among us everyday.

Until we exterminate this breed,

They will kill people of color, while quoting white supremacy.

Because every second I breath.

They are a danger to me.

And they pollute my country.

With hypocrisy, hate, and greed.

A sickness that is triggered at the sight of black skin,

Brown eyes,

Negro,

Black,

Coil,

Curl,

Melanin,

Negroid,

Afro,

Monkey,

Nigger,

So they must pull the trigger.

The disease they preach is only getting bigger.

Painting pictures of God as a white man,

Who approves when the barrel of their gun is pointed at my body

targeting the beating organ in my chest,

That will spread into a red badge of courage against the brown of my

flesh,

And when my head hits the concrete, my fingertips will be a pale

blueprint of what could of been something better to them.

Something worth sparing.

But will only be a reminder of what I will never be,

As they return home to reproduce their hateful mentalities onto the

bodies of their white babies, who will detach from the umbilical cords of

their fair haired mothers,

And the umbilical cord of hate and racism will latch onto their backs and

suck the humanity from the extending tendrils of their hearts,

as they mature into grown bodies,

And try on the pointed white masks that their father's once wore,

Where they can stare at the inferior from it's swollen holes,

And compare the light of their skin to the white of their capes.

A new generation of racism is being allowed to breed,

As we sleep.

They aren't underground, or a secret society.

Many live in a big white house,

Made by slaves,

Many drive around in blue uniforms,

Passed down by their overseer ancestors,

Many are crouching blue eyed babies in the attics of their veteran fathers.

But all I can ask myself is "who's going to save them?"

But the better question is.

Who's going to save them from themselves.

When the rest of the world has had enough.

Negash

Stone faces.

Golden cases.

Carvings of the many eras,

Of the dark races.

Historical places,

Silver ages,

And sacred pages.

Written by the ancestors,

Of the young tar babies,

In cages.

Preserved bodies,

Marble lobbies,

Teachers who became Gods,

Preachers carrying sacred rods,

Star readers,

Empire leaders,

Tribal healers.

Grandiose temples,

Displaying text of the dark race.

Ancient books,

Describing the genius of their reverent grace.

Black man,

Black woman,

Buried in chambers of gold.

Black child,

Black gods,

Built into monuments of stone,

Standing over Africa's heart.

Sitting above Asia's throne.

And inspiring Europe's art.

Black man,

Black woman,

With slant eyes,

Thick lips,

Straight nose,

Nappy hair,

Round hips,

Broad nose,

Wavy hair,

Thin lips.

Some even fair.

Tell me,

That a people who had left physical proof,

Of their undeniable reverie,

Did not foretell,

The heinous genocide,

Of slavery?

And in the response,

To the prophecy of the black holocaust,

Where their descendants would be forced,

So far,

The ancestors,

Left written text,

Carved in stone,

And monuments,

That would stand for generations,

Of black men and women,

On a throne.

So that when we would be lost,

So far,

All we had to do was read the written text,

And behold the monuments,

Of Kings with skin like tar,

And then,

We would remember who we are.

Nothing but Gods.

Fire Spittin

Eyes on the dragon.

Fire spittin flames.

Can't rain on me,

I eat coal and sleep on bedstone.

Where I rest with my gold,

Is a truth never to be told.

Speak now before you sell your soul,

Fire spittin flames,

Forge fire,

Steel pen in the hot rocks,

Boiled temperature,

Overheated.

Never concreted.

Fire spittin flames,

Will never tell their names.

Eyes on the dragon.

But you forgot the prize.

Is what she hides.

Beware her spines,

Or get eaten alive.

Her pen writes the living,

And exposes the death,

Beware her boiling hot fire breath.

She breathes out smoke,

That singes their ears,

Fire spittin dragon,

Steams her tears.

God's breath

You offer me,

Peace and tranquility.

Within your elegant streams,

Lapping against soft powdered cheeks,

Little granules of perfection,

The scent of salt bathes my nostrils,

Taking me home.

With the beats of seagull wings.

And the crashing of foam and spray.

Sipping on rays of sunshine,

Long as my eyelashes.

The song of God's Air,

Replays in my ears.

Singing me into a dream.

Of peace and tranquility.

Here I belong,

Only judged by the sea.

Only black to the sun.

Only flawed to God.

Black Hollywood

If life was a hollywood movie.

Martin Luther King would rise from his casket.

Malcolm X would pluck bullets from gun barrels,

Assata Shakur would bend lies.

Nat Turner would slit lynching ropes with his fingertips.

Eldridge Cleaver would fly to the white house with a bomb.

John Brown would be rising slaves from the dead to free his body.

Emmett Till would be laughing at his kitchen table.

Trayvon Martin would be counting skittles with his mother.

Che Guevera would be painting portraits in Cuba.

If life was a hollywood movie.

I would stop bullets and smell racism.

The police would fear the fire spreading across my shoulders.

Scourged by freedom.

But evil rules the world.

And heroes die.

Where hate is bred,

And love is a lie.

Even today I could say goodbye.

Because hollywood is not waiting for me outside.

But if life was like hollywood scenes.

I'd be writing a different poem.

About my rice and beans.

Broken Bone Alley

Alone and grown,

Death calls my phone,

I choke on the words that tell my story,

Life taunts my bloodstream.

That runs like intricate seams.

Slipping beneath the waves inside a bottle.

To small for my own bones.

Alone and grown.

Choking on plumes of smoke.

Death calls my phone.

She sings my momma's lullaby.

A soothing song,

For someone who is alone and grown.

Too hungry for bread,

Never to be her child again.

Music of the Dying

Voice is high

Though word is low,

Why sing at all,

If you have no flow.

No soul to grow.

The microphone spits,

the lines you sold.

Written behind closed doors,

By a man who just don't know.

But the money gives you hope,

Dangled by rope,

So the microphone,

Becomes an abused hobby,

Among your marble lobby.

So now your voice is high,

But your words are just too low.

How are we supposed to here,

True words of a poet.

But the money still flows,

So who cares about a message.

Glimmer but no grammar,

Bling, bling, bling.

Your voice is high, but I've never heard you sing.

You saying something,

In the recording booth,

Claiming it's music,

Cuz you got gold in your tooth.

But I can't hear your tone.

Cuz your voice is too high,

And your word is too low.

.

P.O.W.E.R

Political words vested in me.

Organized by the footsteps of my heroines.

Womanized the world one vocal cord at a time.

Educated the world of true freedom and justice.

Revolution flows through my bloodstream.

Battle Cry

Am I wrong?

To raise a fist and sing a freedom song,

When they break down my door,

And deny my rights?

They chase me out the country,

When I pick up the fight.

But why should I run?

When I can pick up the gun,

and defend myself as a human being,

Please don´t believe the headlines,

When they pay for my funeral fines.

I defended my body,

My mind,

My right,

to live,

to be,

Am I wrong?

Am I right?

To bend on my knees and pray to God to spare me.

To make my skin an invisible piece of me.

To make my hair long and wavy,

To make my eyes blue like the sky and sea,

When they take me,

I´ll be Black.

And I will paint Black Queens on the wall of my prison cell.

If they do not kill me.

And the revolution will feed me soul and energy.

When they take me.

For you better believe I´m taking at least five of them with me.

And the sky will be fire lit.

Your either against or a part of it.

Cuz there ain´t no freedom in surrender.

Can you dig it?

A Letter From The People

Dear America, we hear you are sending the three-headed dragon onto the brown skinned people of the Middle East,

I have been informed through your bias media outlets that glorify your hateful propaganda.

I have been informed that from the safety and privilege of our White house, that was built on the scarred backs of my ancestors, you seek to inflict more destruction onto the people of Syria.

As if you have not committed enough heinous crimes here on American soil.

Dear America I ask if you had received the consent of the people before sending weapons of mass destruction overseas onto the people of Syria.

I know I was not part of any majority vote.

I cast no ballot onto the election of terrorism and corruption in the heart of my own country.

Yet the disease of hate you have chosen to corrupt Syria with will contaminate the hearts of every person there, and that hate will forever strip the American people of any goodwill or morality in the eyes of the many children who have had their parents blown before their eyes.

As if you had not already contaminated the world with your crimes of colonialism, racism, and exploitation.

You have forced me to witness the horrors of this country that my parents have warned me about for so many years, with my very own eyes.

Dear America, I write this to you because while your president blows his trumpets of corruption and war from his dining table, alongside his French and British conspirators, many more of us including the people of Syria are forced to suffer. Day in and day out.

Dear America, was all the wealth and land you reaped from the crimes of slavery and colonialism not enough?

Now you must work alongside the founding father countries of slavery to inflict more hatred and misery onto the world.

Mr Trump has excited the mobs of racism and has inspired them to light their torches.

The skin of white liberalism is shedding and is exposing the preachers of racism at our jobs, our local coffee shops and waffle houses, outside our lawns, in our schools, in our courtrooms, in our security, and God forbid in the seats of our government.

Dear America, though I do not appreciate the way you terrorize my people, I cannot blame you entirely.

You're merely following in the footsteps of your forefathers.

The reapers of slavery and hatred.

You are merely following in the footsteps of self destruction.

I only ask America, that you do not drag us with you.

I ask this because even though we have been oppressed for more than 400 years we have never become our oppressors.

For if we had, there would be no more white people.

We have become something new.

We have become the last hope of the United States of America.

Therefore America, I can only say what has been said for many years.

The Power belongs to the People.

None of your declarations of dependence or emancipation proclamations can grant me that which God has already given me.

And though you have declined our prepositions over and over again,

I ask of you America, to admit the wrongs of your foundation and to help us build a new one.

To expel the terrorists that control our power houses.

To pay my mother as much as you paid my father, who you did not pay as much as that white man.

To let us walk on our lawns with a phone in our hand,

To let us sell CD's and cigarettes if we want to,

To let us drive while Black,

To let us build our own Black foundations,

To interpret justice in the prison system, for they are humans too,

To punish racists wearing the blue uniform appropriately, whether the victim is black, brown, or white.

To stop flooding our communities with drugs, guns, and pigs,

To promote justice, equality, love, and respect.

Dear America, I write this proposal knowing you will decline it and the wishes of the people you oppress.

As your forefathers did.

And if this is done then we must revert to the ways of "our" forefathers and foremothers as well.

And I can promise repercussions for the denial of our rights as human beings,

The repercussion that were the only driving force behind the enforcement of justice and freedom in America since slavery.

Dear America I feel as though I must remind you, because it seems like you have forgotten that which you have forced us to never forget.

We plucked the cotton,

We built the railroads,

The factories,

The White house,

We labored in the plantations that brought you and your descendants

over decades of wealth,

We raised your babies while you sold ours,

We shredded the sugar cane,

The tobacco,

We went to war with the British,

With the confederates,

With the KKK,

With Vietnam,

And the racist government.

And we have survived with no reparations.

And so as America has declared war on the world,

With the consent of majority vote,

As you have declined your last hope,

The people have decided to wage their own war on this land of

oppression, racism, and sexism,

Home of the incarcerated,

Here my home America,

And we will fight the ruling power until a single generation is free from

the racism of this decadent country,

By any means necessary.

Until we clean house.

With much love and devotion for justice,

In loving memory of Stephon Clarke,

Sandra Bland.

Alton Sterling,

Trayvon Martin,

Freddie Gray,

Tamir Rice,

Emmett till,

Malcolm X,

Winnie Mandela,

Martin Luther King,

And a thousand others.

God bless the oppressed people of America.

God bless Syria and the Middle East,

God bless Africa,

God bless Puerto Rico,

God bless Flint Michigan,

God bless Standing rock,

And yet again, a thousand others,

From the speaker of the people,

Yours truly,

Toni Van Sluytman.

Preacher Man

Preacher, preacher,

What you preaching today?

I saw another mannish boy get arrested yesterday for Black walking,

I saw another sista get slammed to the ground for Black talking,

The prostitutes, the drug pushers, and the junkies threaten my family,

The white man my mother works for calls her mammy,

The pigs follow me to my job every day,

The landlord won't listen to a word I say.

So what you preaching today preacher man?

Check after check, but I'm still not allowed on whitey's deck.

My money's running low, so I suppose God is the last place to go.

I slip you my cash, even though I know it won't last,

If the landlord, pigs, and the government want my money why not the

Lord to?

So preacher man go ahead and stand at the altar and do what you do.

I lost my brother to drive by the other day,

So preacher man now what you gotta say?

Your flyers say you can make it all go away,

Mr Preacher man.

So Mr Preacher man what you preaching today?

Is it about the God who died for the sins of I?

When the sinners eat steak and pees after they steal and lie.

Mr Preacher man when I handed you my money I think they thought it funny,

Cuz the next day my water was cut off by your buddy,

He went by the name of Mr Sunny.

I asked for the hand of God to spare my brother Rod,

Every day I write him a letter,

When I asked Preacher man what to do,

He said pray for things to get better.

Giving up pennies a day,

To hear Mr Preacher Man pray,

So Preacher man what you preaching today?

He gives me bitter tears before leaving to his mansion on Broadway,

Another week of waiting for things to change,

The other day I heard strange sounds outside my home,

Was it God's plan to leave me in this world alone?

There goes the sounds "Pow Pow" outside the church,

POW POW

Mr Preacher man. So Mr Preacher man what you got to preach now?

Syria

My parents promised me an age,

But it was stolen from a country of rage,

Soul mistaken by violence's wrath,

Smoke and guns riddle my path,

Walking on concrete roads,

Of broken glass,

Clouds of black smoke,

Shooting into the sky,

So fast.

My parents promised me an age,

But now I can't find them inside this cage.

My toy soldiers turned into venomous monsters,

Threatening to choke my lungs.

I camouflaged into the misery,

Barefoot in the fiery pits of hell,

Nothing is left to smell,

I saw a picture of a blonde white man,

Waving from a white house,

I saw the blood of my parents greasing his palms,

I shouted their name but no one ever came,

He just kept smiling with a wave,

I smelled the violence light up the air,

The sky became the ground in a brilliant shatter,

At this point my name didn't even matter,

I stared at my reflection,

Hoping that strange dirty little girl can point me in the right direction,

She is the only one who can see me,

Not as a victim of violence,

But a survivor in a dying world,

Though how much longer can I survive,

Will anyone care if I die?

Survivor?

Victim?

I wondered which one they'd call me.

And so I decided to ask the venom monsters,

One spat and called me a savage,

I asked what do they call me,

He laughed and said,

"You are collateral damage"

Aunt June

Sleepless nights left in your embrace,

Whispering forgotten songs from the lands of a sacred race,

Trekking across plantations, she was saying to me,

But hear I say,

Nah mama I don't look like her,

Nah mama you can agree wouldn't you say?

Hey hey, lil mae,

You're black now,

Mama would say.

I had hair like Aunt June,

Skin like a prune,

Eyes big like the moon,

Lips swollen like fool.

And I say,

Nah mama I'll grow out of it,

I'll live out of my skin,

I can learn to blend mama.

Nah mama,

Nah.

He took me to the sea,

A lover so sweet to me,

I read him Uncle Sam's poetry,

He talked about the slave and the shack,

I ask,

Nah, what that got to do with me?

He said he loved me cuz I was black.

Denial,

He said he saw me in the Nile.

There I left my Satan.

Standing too black for the white of my eye.

Nah boy, I don't kiss like her.

No, No, No,

I spoke to God one day,

Asking how is this fair?

Why I couldn't be fare?

She said,

Aw lil mae,

You have hair like Aunt June,

Skin like a prune,

Eyes big like the moon,

Lips swollen like a fool.

Nah God, I don't sound like her.

I work real hard,

But can't get no money,

My lover is gone,

My grin ain't funny.

I talked to a white woman

I asked her for a hand,

She said something about stolen African land,

Nah, What that got to do with me?

She said,

Aw lil mae,

You have hair like Aunt June,

Skin like a prune,

Eyes big like the moon,

Lips swollen like a fool.

But I,

I don't walk like her.

Nah.

One day I saw Lil Nay,

She said I was black like Aunt June,

That she'd like to look like me soon,

And my skin could carry a tune,

My lips swollen like the moon,

And I say,

Nah Lil Nay,

I don't look like you.

And she said,

Aw lil mae, who you look like then?

I say I never looked in the mirror before,

And I dunno,

Whom I to be.

For I have turned my back on,

My mama,

My lover,

My God,

My white woman,

My lil Nay.

And my Aunt June.

Aunt June.

Because now.

I don't look like her.

Rock n Stone

I can't breathe,

Beneath cotton sheets,

Your arms make me weak,

An ocean beneath your eyes.

I can't breathe,

Your love is so sweet,

My lover is rock,

The surface beneath my feet.

I can't breathe,

With the promise of your blank canvas,

Fill me with tranquility,

Your four edges each with its own personality,

You are rock.

Be my rock,

In my medal ring,

Rock baby,

Rock my world.

Sweet, sweet, like stone.

And I can't breathe,

Can I love you?

Can I hold you?

Can I at least have one thing?

Can I have my rock?

Can I have the ground beneath me,

Can they take away my love?

I can feed you,

I can take care of you,

All forty acres of you.

All I ever wanted,

Was to breath,

All I ever wanted,

Was rock,

And stone,

A lover,

A home,

All I need is some fuel,

And one mule,

And I'll leave ye alone,

Just give me rock,

Rock baby.

Rock.

But it wasn't meant to be,

Cuz they took rock away from me,

My one thing left in life,

Was rock,

Was my rock baby,

They took him away,

They ate my mule,

They used my fuel,

They stole my crops,

And sold it at shops,

And now I ain't have nothing.

And all I wanted,

Was to breath,

All I wanted,

Was rock,

Just give me my rock,

Rock baby,

Rock.

But we weren't meant to be,

So I burnt down everything,

And took rock to the grave with me.

Mother Maker

What were we before we woke up?

Perhaps a more divine entity among many others,

A cell in the body,

A freckle on the cheek,

A grain in the desert,

And what did we call we?

A whisper beyond mentality,

An untouchable physicality,

Precious to the trees,

What were we before we went to sleep?

Perhaps human beings,

I feel severed from the trees,

My nostrils can no longer breath god's air,

I can't taste the honey,

I can no longer embrace the air,

Take me back.

To the days before we woke up,

And became humans,

So I can speak to that which created we,

And ask why does she drop,

The curse of my nature on to me,

So I can ask,

What were we called we?

Before we fell asleep,

And became human beings.

Perhaps when I die,

I will become we again,

I will become that which is greater than me,

And come back a tree.

Because the tree has never adopted,

The wrath of we.

Confessions of a Child of Chain

A day goes by and now I just can't believe it as I lay in my sheets.

When the bang of a gunshot mixes with the sound of weeps

There's another black child laying dead on the streets

Now must I turn my head and be just like a ghost floating among sheep?

Must I stand by as my people fall one by one to the hand of oppression?

This is the part where I walk on by or learn a lesson.

And keep my head turned up to the sky,

So I won't have to remember the crooked position of his arms,

That were most likely raised up as he died.

What's that you say?

There's a riot on the way?

Deep down I'm feeling like a clown,

Driving myself insane trying to explain,

Why, this kid had to die.

Like, what was he doing outside?

Was he drunk, homeless, or high?

But deep down, my heart is trippin inside.

Cuz I keep seeing the same police man driving by.

Giving my people the same ol stink eye.

And now my home don't feel so safe anymore,

I'm wondering if it would be better if I was rich instead of poor.

Or if the pigment in my skin didn't resemble the same shade of brown

As the kid I saw laying dead on the ground.

Maybe if I was lighter,

Or brighter,

Something in that cops eye won't remind of the millions of times,

They had shot,

killed,

And arrested,

Any signs of a Black fighter.

And I can see the outlines of tired eyed old women dressed in black,

Surrounding another casket buried in the back.

And I wonder if maybe that could be me,

Laying so peacefully,

With America's bullet lodged in my chest,

And even if that had not killed me,

The FBI would come for my arrest.

Maybe if I run,

I could escape racisms gun.

I could ignore the screams of my people,

Shattering glass windows with hearts lit up with grief.

No, no.

They'll just drag me to court for the hundredth time.

And gag my mouth and chain my hands,

Like they did to Bobby Seale in 1969.

Or they'll just frame me of a crime if I do not heed them.

Like they did to Assata Shakur because she preached freedom.

And if I pick up the gun to defend myself against the feds,

I'll be called a terrorist, like they called Huey P. Newton,

And they'll have me drugged with meds.

And the day they plan my death,

It'll be a paid black man or woman with a gun pointed to my head,

So they can say it wasn't them,

But my own people instead.

Because that's what they said about Huey when they found him dead.

And if I had a daughter,

I'd have to leave her.

Because they'd chase me out of the country,

Like they did to Eldridge and Kathleen Cleaver.

Not because I'm bad, evil, or kill a lot.

But because I have a gun, I'm Black, and I want justice for that kid they shot.

Who knows, maybe I'm overreacting.

Maybe this phase of anger and grief won't be lasting,

And after they bring the dogs and hoses,

My people will just go home and turn their noses.

Maybe the next time I come to a stop,

I won't have to worry about that red handed cop,

Who keeps on circling my block,

Now wouldn't that be shock.

Maybe I just think too much about death because I'm surrounded by it every day.

Maybe deep down I feel like I'm still an American slave.

Praying every second that I'm not the next body laying under a grave.

I guess what I'm trying to say is that I'm starting to feel like a panther after all,

Because a panther only attacks when it's back is against the wall.

And maybe I wanna pick up the gun.

Cuz God forbid if that kid was ever my son.

Maybe I could scare the cops away,

So my kids can grown, live, and play.

Whom I kidding? I could die anyway.

Because things are different than before,

Now it's down to what you're willing to die for.

Truth be told I'm no revolutionary,

But out in these streets things are getting real scary.

So in my arms a gun I will carry.

This isn't about my neck being on the line,

It's about who's child I'll be saving next time.

And maybe the child will grow up to be a liberator, a teacher, the next

president, or a powerful politician.

But either way God knows I'm on a mission.

And maybe with my sacrifice,

Next time that cop will think twice.

And the next time I see that red handed cop.

He better keep on riding.

Because there is a revolution igniting,

This ain't about being equal.

Because in life this time,

You better believe, I'm gonna die fighting for my people.

Sista Soldier

A little girl once fooled me,

She tried to lie and school me,

And every day I see her in my reflection,

I remember to go in the right direction.

Spanish boy gotta good black gem, he say "baby come give it up to me"

But I say "hey little boy you just gotta go, cause I'm leaving here back to Tennessee"

He say "Baby I can try harder"

I said "Boy don't even bother"

Cuz I remembered who was my father.

Midnight Doves from his Leather Black Gloves

The call of your name,

Just drives me insane,

When I see you walking by,

With a lovely fire in your eyes,

To the sound of hip hop beats,

I hear your voice echo in the streets,

Your beautiful voice could shake the soil of Africa,

And shatter the silence deep in the American ghettos,

When I first saw you. You were one of many photos,

In grey and white,

Breathless, I couldn't shake the power of such a sight.

Black was the color of his hands,

Reaching for an embrace,

His veins like streams from a lake of heaven resting in his eyes,

Black was the color of his hair,

Soft to touch, Oh how I loved it such,

Black was the color of his skin,

I see an African King as I take in,

The beauty of his dark melanin,

In, fascinated, emasculated,

I saw him inside of Nat Turner's bible,

I read his initials all over Harriet Tubman's rifle,

I saw him sitting in an all Black High School,

I saw him swimming in a "Whites Only" swimming pool.

He could never stand still,

But somehow I caught his beauty with a pencil.

I pointed to him and asked a young Black man what did he see.

And he said "I see a Black woman, standing on a mountain and carrying my child in her arms."

Chain Gang Man

Oink, Oink, Bang, Bang

Comes the song of the Chain Gang.

One by One, while they shuffle their feet

Uncle Tom points his gun

as they march down the street.

Oink, Oink, Bang, Bang

Comes the sound of the beat,

One man falls from the line,

Cuz he ain't got nothing to eat.

Left to right, comes the Chain Gang song,

No rights, no love, yet they marching on along.

As the song plays on,

You can hear the police cars,

But it won't be very long,

Till Chain Gang is back behind bars.

Oink, Oink, Bang, Bang.

Yet another man falls,

Beatin to death,

Cuz he was trying to make some calls.

But the Chain Gang can never lag,

So long as they live under the American flag,

So the chains rattle along,

As they move to the song.

Oink, Oink, Bang, Bang.

Comes the cry of a lame man,

Lying on his side,

Drinking medicine out of a beer can.

But no doctor around,

To see if he ever got fed,

So no one questioned it,

When they found him dead.

Oink, Oink, Bang, Bang

Only one more man left on the Chain Gang.

No one ever hears him,

And the pigs always beat him,

And there's never any hope,

Even with a head full of dope.

So now he's out on parole,

And he got no goal.

So he tries to find a gun,

Cuz there ain't nowhere to run.

Oink, Oink, Bang, Bang

No way! No way! Get your head in the game!

Says a woman dressed in black,

In a grey Cadillac,

"You ain't at all fine, and your running out of time, so it's about time

you liberated your mind"

Five years on the line,

No longer serving time,

But the people he will carry.

Cuz Mr Chain Gang man,

Was now a revolutionary.

ABOUT THE AUTHOR

Antoinette Van Sluytman is a seventeen-year-old home schooled
Afro-Latina from California. She has apprenticed under many masters to
become an African American Historian and Artisan. Antoinette was
home schooled by both her parents. Her mother has been a professor of
Interior Architecture for over fifteen years and is a powerful voice in the
Womanist movement. Her father is a Master Artisan and African
American Historian. Together they are the founders of "Obavan Dzine
Studios and Gallery."
Antoinette has had much of her work featured and sold nationally and
internationally since the early age of thirteen. One of her drawings have
been featured and sold at Morgan State University and another featured
at the Pratt University student art exhibition. Antoinette has also won the
2017 "Art and Writing Scholastic National Gold Medal Award for
Drawing" and the "Art and Writing Scholastic Western Region Silver
Key for Poetry."
Antoinette is an advocate for self-love and empowerment and uses her
creative skills to speak out against oppression and racism through
conscious revolutionary art and writing.

Made in the USA
Middletown, DE
15 February 2022

60972358R00066